MACKENZIE POLTERGEIST

This series features unsolved mysteries, urban legends, and other curious stories. Each creepy, shocking, or befuddling book focuses on what people believe and hear. True or not? That's for you to decide!

45th Parallel Press

Published in the United States of America by Cherry Lake Publishing
Ann Arbor, Michigan
www.cherrylakepublishing.com

Author: Virginia Loh-Hagan
Reading Adviser: Marla Conn MS, Ed., Literacy specialist, Read-Ability, Inc.
Book Designer: Felicia Macheske

Photo Credits: © Alina G/Shutterstock.com, cover; © iolya/Shutterstock.com, 5; © Jiri Vaclavek/Shutterstock.com, 7; © Lolostock/Shutterstock.com, 8; © iolya/Shutterstock.com, 11; © dourleak/Shutterstock.com, 13; © Saida Shigapova/Shutterstock.com, 15; © Sergey Goryachev/Shutterstock.com, 16; © Discha-AS/Shutterstock.com, 18; © Photographee.eu/Shutterstock.com, 21; © eakkaluktemwanich/Shutterstock.com, 22; © Arman Zhenikeyev/Shutterstock.com, 25; © Sukpaiboonwat/Shutterstock.com, 26; © By withGod/Shutterstock.com, 29

Graphic Elements Throughout: © iofoto/Shutterstock.com; © COLCU/Shutterstock.com; © spacedrone808/Shutterstock.com; © rf.vector.stock/Shutterstock.com; © donatas1205/Shutterstock.com; © cluckva/Shutterstock.com; © Eky Studio/Shutterstock.com

45th Parallel Press is an imprint of Cherry Lake Publishing.

Library of Congress Cataloging-in-Publication Data

Names: Loh-Hagan, Virginia, author.
Title: MacKenzie poltergeist / by Dr. Virginia Loh-Hagan.
Description: Ann Arbor : Cherry Lake Publishing, 2018. | Series: Urban Legends: Don't read alone! | Includes bibliographical references and index. | Audience: Grades 4 to 6.
Identifiers: LCCN 2017033731| ISBN 9781534107687 (hardcover) | ISBN 9781534109667 (pdf) | ISBN 9781534108677 (pbk.) | ISBN 9781534120655 (hosted ebook)
Subjects: LCSH: Greyfriars Kirkyard (Edinburgh, Scotland)—Juvenile literature. | Poltergeists—Scotland—Edinburgh—Juvenile literature.
Classification: LCC BF1483 .L64 2018 | DDC 133.1/294134—dc23
LC record available at https://lccn.loc.gov/2017033731

Cherry Lake Publishing would like to acknowledge the work of The Partnership for 21st Century Skills. Please visit *www.p21.org* for more information.

Printed in the United States of America
Corporate Graphics

TABLE OF CONTENTS

Chapter One

WAKING UP THE DEAD

What happened in 1998? What is a mausoleum?

It was 1998. There was a heavy rain in Edinburgh. Edinburgh is the capital of Scotland. A homeless man needed **shelter**. Shelters are places that protect people from bad weather. The man went to a **cemetery**. Cemeteries are where dead bodies are buried. He broke into a **mausoleum**. Mausoleums are tombs. They're special burial places. They have little rooms. Dead bodies are in these rooms.

The tomb was dark. The man felt around. He opened a door. He walked down stairs. He went into another room. He saw four wooden **coffins**. Coffins are containers for dead bodies. The man was hungry. He needed money. He smashed open the coffins. He was hoping to find fancy things to sell.

Traditionally, families are buried together in mausoleums.

CONSIDER THE
EVIDENCE

Edinburgh is known as one of the most haunted cities in the world. It has a history of violent rulers. Its people believe in witches and ghosts. There are many haunted spots. Greyfriars Cemetery is one of them. It was established in 1562. The land was originally used as a garden by monks. Over 500,000 burials are recorded there. That's a lot of dead bodies. In time, the area filled with bodies and became a hill. It rose 15 feet (4.6 meters). The soil is thin. Sometimes bones rise to the top. People say they see things that aren't there. They say they see ghosts. They say they see white birds. They say they see children.

The floor gave way. The man fell into a deep pit. Years before, the area was a **plague** pit. A plague is a sickness. There was a Black Death. This was a time when sickness killed many people. There wasn't enough room to bury the bodies. People dumped bodies into this pit. They covered it up.

In the tomb, the bodies were sealed up. They hadn't broken down. The homeless man saw human bones. He saw rotting human skin. He saw green slime. He smelled death. He screamed. He clawed his way out. He ran away. He cut his head on the door. Blood dripped down his face.

Bodies that are buried correctly will decompose, or break down.

Some people believe strange things happen around cemeteries.

A guard was walking his dog. He heard strange noises. He saw the homeless man running away. He got scared. He ran away, too. The next day, he told everyone what happened. Then, he quit.

No one saw the homeless man again. But they say he woke up evil forces. People started getting hurt. A few days afterward, a woman looked into the tomb. She was blasted by cold air. She fell backward. Another woman passed out next to the tomb. Bruises covered her neck. Dead animals were found around the tomb. The city closed off the area.

Chapter Two

THE BLACK MAUSOLEUM

Who is buried in the Black Mausoleum? Where is the Black Mausoleum? What is a poltergeist?

The homeless man was at the Black Mausoleum. This is a **vaulted** tomb. Vaulted means to have arched ceilings. The tomb's door has a chain and lock. This holds the doors shut. This tomb was the final resting place of "Bloody" MacKenzie. MacKenzie and his family are buried there.

The tomb is in Edinburgh. The tomb is in Greyfriars Cemetery. It's behind high walls. It's behind locked gates. It's in an area called the **Covenanter's** Prison. Covenanters were a religious group in Scotland.

In Scotland, the cemetery is known as "Greyfriars Kirkyard."

SPOTLIGHT

BIOGRAPHY

Jan-Andrew Henderson was born in 1962. He was born in Scotland. He studied journalism at Napier University. He studied English and philosophy at Edinburgh University. He visited the United States. He spent 7 years there. He had many different jobs. He was a rubber stamp designer. He was an Easter bunny. He acted in children's theater. He returned to Edinburgh. He got a job as a ghost tour guide. He said, "Tourists kept asking me questions I didn't know the answers to. So I figured I'd better learn. And, in the process, I discovered I loved history!" He became an expert on the MacKenzie Poltergeist. He wrote books about it. He created his own ghost tour company. His tour is called "City of the Dead."

There was evil around the Black Mausoleum. Some people believe the homeless man released the MacKenzie **Poltergeist**. Poltergeists are a type of ghost. They move things. They make loud noises. They hurt people. They haunt people and places. They cause trouble.

The MacKenzie Poltergeist is different from others. First, there are a lot of reports. Many people report experiencing the poltergeist. They feel hot spots. They feel cold spots. They see white figures. They smell weird things. They hear strange things. Second, the incidents are serious. People get hurt. They've fainted. They've been cut. They've been hit.

People say they hear knocking noises under the ground and inside the tomb.

Chapter Three

BLOODY MACKENZIE

Who is Sir George MacKenzie? What happened to the Covenanters? Why was MacKenzie known as "Bloody" MacKenzie?

Some people think the MacKenzie Poltergeist lives in the Black Mausoleum. But it's not the ghost of MacKenzie. It's the combined evil forces around him.

Bloody MacKenzie is Sir George MacKenzie. He was born around 1636. He died in 1691. He was a lawyer. At first, he defended Covenanters. Then later, he mistreated them. He was known to be cruel. In all, he was responsible for killing 18,000 people.

The Covenanters were a Scottish Presbyterian group. They formed in the 17th century. They signed the National **Covenant** in 1638. Covenant means agreement. The Covenanters defended their religion. They didn't want to change religions.

Religious freedom means being free to practice whatever religion you want.

King Charles II wanted people to pledge loyalty to him.

Charles II wanted to be king. He signed the National Covenant to get support. He became king of the Scots. Then, he betrayed the Covenanters. He lied. He started killing them. The Covenanters fought back. There was a war. It lasted 50 years. It was called the Killing Times.

The Battle of Bothwell Bridge took place on June 22, 1679. The Covenanters lost. More than 3,000 were taken prisoner. They were sent to Edinburgh. About 400 were held at the place that is now Greyfriars Cemetery. They were kept in an open area. It became known as Covenanters' Prison.

Some say the prison was the first concentration camp.

MacKenzie was in charge of the prisoners. He didn't give them enough food. He gave them a small bit of bread each day. He starved them. He didn't protect them against the weather. He kept them out in the open. He hanged some of them. He shot some of them. He beheaded some of them. He put their heads on walls around the city. He tortured some in public. He sold some as slaves. Many men got sick. About 150 men died. The survivors were sent to Australia.

The dead were buried at Covenanters' Prison. MacKenzie was later buried near their graves. It's strange to have him buried close to the people he killed.

REAL-WORLD
CONNECTION

Some people believe in the "*Poltergeist* curse." *Poltergeist* is a series of movies. The movies are about poltergeists haunting a family. The first movie was released in 1982. Several of the movie's stars died. Dominique Dunne played the oldest daughter. She died in 1982. She was age 22. She was strangled by her boyfriend. Heather O'Rourke played the little girl. She died in 1988. She was age 12. She had stomach and heart problems. Other stars died. Lou Perryman died in 2009. He was killed with an ax. Julian Beck died in 1985. He died of stomach cancer. Will Sampson died in 1987. He died of kidney failure.

Chapter Four

EVIL, EVIL EVERYWHERE

How was the MacKenzie Poltergeist formed?
Who is Colin Grant?

Some people think the graves are too close. MacKenzie was the killer. The Covenanters were his **victims**. Victims are people who get hurt by others. For 300 years, killer and victims rested close to each other. This created evil forces. This created the MacKenzie Poltergeist.

People tried to get rid of the evil. An **exorcist** came. Exorcists are people trained to cast out evil. They're usually priests. Colin Grant was an exorcist.

He went to the Black Mausoleum in 1999. He said there were several demons there. He died in 2000. He had a heart attack. People think the MacKenzie Poltergeist killed him.

An exorcism was performed at the cemetery.

Greyfriars became a scary place. Teenagers go there on dares. They go to the Black Mausoleum. They knock on the door. They do this three times. They yell, "Bloody MacKenzie! Come out if you dare! Lift the **sneck** and draw the bar." Then, they run away. Sneck means a door latch.

In 2003, teenagers snuck into the Black Mausoleum. They stole a head. They used it as a ball. They used it as a puppet. The head was later found. It was brought back to the tomb. The teenagers were arrested. But this act was upsetting. People think this made the MacKenzie Poltergeist more evil.

Sometimes cameras don't work around the Black Mausoleum.

INVESTIGATION TIPS

- Ignore poltergeists. Don't give them any attention.

- If you must talk to poltergeists, talk nicely.

- Host a séance. Sit down with someone who can talk to ghosts.

- Practice "smudging." This is a Native American ritual. Tie a bunch of sage together. Light it on fire. Burn it slowly. Let the smoke go all over. This gets rid of evil forces.

- Get holy things. Examples are holy water, crosses, and Bibles. Place them around the area. This wards off evil forces.

- Sprinkle salt around the room. This will protect you.

- Study geomancy. This is the paranormal study of Earth's energies. Poltergeists disrupt Earth's energies.

- Hold iron. Iron weakens poltergeists.

Chapter Five

GHOSTLY REASONS

How do pheromones create a belief in the MacKenzie Poltergeist?

Odd things happen around Greyfriars Cemetery. Some people blame the MacKenzie Poltergeist. Some believe in scientific reasons.

One reason is **pheromones**. These are chemicals. They come out of living things. They affect actions and behaviors. This is most common in insects. Humans are also affected by these chemical signals.

Some think the Black Mausoleum has a lot of emotions. It has emotions from the prisoners. It has emotions from MacKenzie. It also has emotions from the visitors. Visitors tour the area. They hear the stories. They get upset. This causes people to feel sick. This makes them think they feel ghosts.

Emotions include fear and apprehension.

Electric energy comes from machines like this.

There are other explanations for how people feel around the tomb. Some blame high-**voltage** machinery. Voltage is electricity. Edinburgh University has a computer lab. The lab is behind the Black Mausoleum. It has many machines. These machines give off energy. Some people are sensitive to this energy. This energy may make them see things. It may make them feel things. People may think these things are related to ghosts. They trick their minds. They hear ghost stories. They want to believe.

EXPLAINED BY SCIENCE

People try to make sense of things they can't explain. Christopher French is a professor of psychology. He works at the University of London. He said, "People assume that if they cannot explain something in natural terms, then it must be something paranormal." There are many scientific reasons for believing in ghosts. Some people have sleep problems. They see hallucinations. Hallucinations are fake images. People think these images are ghosts. Some people have pareidolia. This is when people see a pattern where there isn't one. For example, some people see faces in things. This causes them to think they see ghosts.

Another reason lies deep underground. Sandstone is the rock underneath the cemetery. Sandstone has pores. Pores are small openings. Mineral water could flow into the pores. It would cause many small chemical reactions. This could cause a little shake. This creates an electrical field. This could affect people.

Groups of people think they see the same things. They think they feel the same things. They combine their stories. They create their own truths.

Real or not? It doesn't matter. The MacKenzie Poltergeist lives in people's imaginations.

Sandstone is far below the buried bodies.

DID YOU KNOW?

Black Hart Entertainment is a company. It runs the ghost tours at Greyfriars Cemetery. It keeps records. It keeps photographs. It keeps track of visitors' injuries.

Greyfriars Cemetery is also famous for the Greyfriars Bobby. This is a bronze statue. It's of a dog. The statue guards the cemetery. The dog was loyal. Its owner died. It stood guard over the owner's grave. It did this for 14 years. Then, it died. It was buried close to its owner.

Greyfriars has a grave for Thomas Ridell. Ridell was the inspiration for Tom Riddle. Riddle is a famous character in the Harry Potter books.

Greyfriars is close to Elephant House Café. This is where J. K. Rowling wrote the first lines of Harry Potter. She sat in a window seat overlooking the cemetery.

The ghost tour at Greyfriars Cemetery has a warning. The warning reads, "The MacKenzie Poltergeist can cause physical and mental distress. You join the tour at your own risk."

Jan-Andrew Henderson lived near Greyfriars Cemetery. A fire hit his house in 2003. It destroyed everything he had on the MacKenzie Poltergeist. No other houses were damaged.

John Haynes was a criminal. He hid in the Black Mausoleum. He hid for 6 months. The police found him. Haynes was insane. He said the coffins moved at night. He said he heard MacKenzie.

CONSIDER THIS!

Take a Position: Learn about other poltergeists. Do you think poltergeists are real? Why or why not? Argue your point with reasons and evidence.

Say What? Reread chapter 3. Learn more about Sir George MacKenzie. Explain why people consider him to be brutal.

Think About It! Would you visit Greyfriars Cemetery? Do you think you'd be scared? Challenge yourself to take a local ghost tour.

LEARN MORE

- Loh-Hagan, Virginia. *Ghost Hunter: Odd Jobs*. Ann Arbor, MI: Cherry Lake Publishing, 2016.

- McCollum, Sean. *Handbook to Ghosts, Poltergeists, and Haunted Houses*. North Mankato, MN: Capstone Press, 2017.

- Stone, Adam. *Ghosts*. Minneapolis: Bellwether Media, 2011.

GLOSSARY

cemetery (SEM-ih-ter-ee) a place where dead bodies are buried

coffins (KAW-finz) containers for dead bodies

covenant (KUHV-uh-nuhnt) contract or agreement

covenanter (KUHV-uh-nuhnt-er) a religious group in Scotland

exorcist (EKS-ur-sist) a person who is trained to cast out evil

mausoleum (maw-zuh-LEE-uhm) special burial places or tombs that have their own little rooms

pheromones (FER-uh-mohnz) chemical signals that affect behaviors

plague (PLAYG) sickness that kills a lot of people

poltergeist (POHL-tur-gyest) a type of ghost that causes trouble

shelter (SHEL-tur) place with a roof that protects people from the weather

sneck (SNEK) Scottish phrase for door latch

vaulted (VAWLT-id) a room that has arched ceilings

victims (VIK-tuhmz) people who get hurt by others

voltage (VOHL-tij) electricity

INDEX

ABOUT THE AUTHOR

Dr. Virginia Loh-Hagan is an author, university professor, former classroom teacher, and curriculum designer. She believes in ghosts. She lives in San Diego with her very tall husband and very naughty dogs. To learn more about her, visit www.virginialoh.com.